Jobs If You Like...

Animals

Charlotte Guillain

Raintree

www.raintreepublishers.co.uk
Visit our website to find out more information about Raintree books.

To order:

☎ Phone 0845 6044371

🖹 Fax +44 (0) 1865 312263

💻 Email myorders@raintreepublishers.co.uk

Customers from outside the UK please telephone +44 1865 312262

Raintree is an imprint of Capstone Global Library Limited, a company incorporated in England and Wales having its registered office at 7 Pilgrim Street, London, EC4V 6LB – Registered company number: 6695582

Text © Capstone Global Library Limited 2013
First published in hardback in 2013
The moral rights of the proprietor have been asserted.

Edited by Rebecca Rissman, Daniel Nunn, and Adrian Vigliano
Designed by Steve Mead
Picture research by Mica Brancic
Originated by Capstone Global Library Ltd
Printed and bound in China by South China Printing Company

ISBN 978 1 406 24062 7 (hardback)
16 15 14 13 12
10 9 8 7 6 5 4 3 2 1

British Library Cataloguing in Publication Data
Guillain, Charlotte.
Jobs for kids who like animals.
590.2'3-dc22
A full catalogue record for this book is available from the British Library.

Acknowledgements
We would like to thank the following for permission to reproduce photographs: [select]

Cover photograph of [select] reproduced with permission of [select].

We would like to thank [name of organization or individual] for [pronoun] invaluable help in the preparation of this book.

Every effort has been made to contact copyright holders of material reproduced in this book. Any omissions will be rectified in subsequent printings if notice is given to the publisher.

Disclaimer
All the Internet addresses (URLs) given in this book were valid at the time of going to press. However, due to the dynamic nature of the Internet, some addresses may have changed, or sites may have changed or ceased to exist since publication. While the author and publisher regret any inconvenience this may cause readers, no responsibility for any such changes can be accepted by either the author or the publisher.

Contents

Why do animals matter? 4

Be a vet 6

Be a farmer 8

Be a zookeeper 10

Be an entomologist 12

Be a police dog handler 14

Be a wildlife biologist 16

Be an animal welfare inspector 18

Be an animal care assistant 20

Be a riding instructor 22

Be an assistance dog trainer 24

Choosing the right job for you 26

Animal job chart 28

Glossary 30

Find out more 31

Index 32

Some words are shown in bold, **like this**. You can find out what they mean by looking in the glossary.

Why do animals matter?

Do you love animals? Are you interested in wild animals? Do you have pets? Animals are important to humans in many different ways.

Many people enjoy spending time with their pets.

Protecting wild animals is very important work.

Some animals, such as assistance dogs, help people. Other animals are an important part of the natural world and need to be protected. There are lots of exciting jobs that involve animals. Read this book to find out more.

Be a vet

If you were a vet, you would save animals' lives! You would help **injured** and sick animals and give others medicine to stay healthy. You might help to make new medicines for animals.

Vets often look after people's pets.

Vets need to be able to work out what is wrong, because animals can't tell them!

Vets need to like animals because they work with them all the time. Vets also need to be good at talking to animals' owners. They have to explain how to care for animals properly.

Be a farmer

If you were a farmer, you might keep cows for milk or sheep for wool. You might keep chickens for eggs. Some farmers have unusual animals, such as ostriches or llamas!

Farmers know how to look after hens so they will lay lots of eggs.

Farmers have to take good care of their animals and make sure they are all healthy. They need to be able to move their animals around safely and feed them properly. Many farmers have grown up on farms and are used to farm animals.

Farmers use special equipment, for example, for milking cows.

Be a zookeeper

Would you like to take care of elephants? If you were a zookeeper, it would be your job to feed and care for amazing animals. You would clean out their homes and talk to visitors about the zoo's animals.

Zookeepers know how to look after many types of animals.

Many zoos now help to protect rare animals.

Zookeepers have to know what animals need to be healthy. They are comfortable **handling** many types of animals, including dangerous ones! They also care about protecting nature and wildlife.

Be an entomologist

If you like insects then you could be an entomologist! Entomologists study insects and how they affect humans. They might learn about insects that make us ill or insects that help our food crops to grow.

Many people study bees and other important insects.

Entomologists love learning about bugs!

Some entomologists study insects outside in nature. Others work in a **laboratory** or teach other people about insects. Many entomologists become **experts** on one type of insect.

Be a police dog handler

If you were a police dog handler, you and your dog might rescue people in trouble. You might find bombs or other dangerous things before they hurt people. Or your dog might catch criminals!

Police dog handlers and their dogs get to know each other very well.

Police dogs start training when they are very young!

Police dog handlers can look after their dogs from when they are puppies. The dogs often live with their handlers and they train together every day. Dog handlers have to feed, exercise, and care for their dogs.

Be a wildlife biologist

If you were a wildlife biologist, you would spend a lot of time studying wild birds and animals. You might also study animals' **habitats**. You would collect information and tell other people about it.

Wildlife biologists can spend time living in the wild with rare and beautiful animals.

Wildlife biologists study wildlife in all types of habitats.

Wildlife biologists often work outside in nature. They can become **experts** on one type of bird or animal. Some wildlife biologists work in **conservation** to protect wildlife and habitats.

Be an animal welfare inspector

Do you think people should look after animals properly? If you were an animal welfare inspector, your job would be to make sure this happened. You would visit animals and check that they are happy and healthy.

This horse is getting the care it needs.

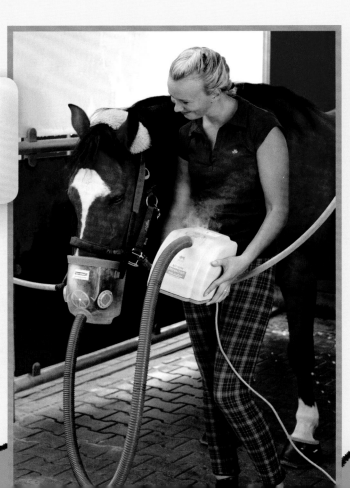

Animal welfare inspectors work with farmers to make sure farm animals are well cared for.

Animal welfare inspectors rescue animals when they get an **emergency** call. Sometimes they help people and tell them how to look after their pets. They can work with all types of animals, from rabbits to snakes!

Be an animal care assistant

What happens to animals that are rescued? If you were an animal care assistant, you would look after them at an animal centre. You would feed and clean the animals and make sure they are healthy.

Care assistants look after animals that need help.

Animal care assistants play with rescue dogs and take them for walks. They sometimes train the dogs, too. They try to find the animals new owners who are caring and suitable.

Care assistants help rescue dogs get ready for a new family.

Be a riding instructor

Do you love horses? If you were a riding instructor, you would work with horses every day! You could help riders train for competitions, such as the Olympics.

If you were a riding instructor, you might teach people who have never ridden horses before.

Some riding instructors help disabled children enjoy riding horses.

Riding instructors have to be good at riding horses so they can show people what to do. They need to be good at teaching and make sure everyone is safe. Sometimes riding instructors also help to look after the horses.

Be an assistance dog trainer

Would you like a job working with dogs? If you were an assistance dog trainer, you would train dogs to help disabled people. You would start working with puppies and find **volunteers** to take them for walks.

Assistance dogs start training when they are puppies.

When the puppies grow up, assistance dog trainers give them special training. This teaches the dogs to help **visually impaired** people move around, or let deaf people know when they hear important sounds.

The dog trainer matches each dog to an owner and trains them together.

Choosing the right job for you

When you decide what you want to do when you grow up, don't just think about school subjects. Think about what you enjoy doing. If you think insects are creepy then you wouldn't like being an entomologist!

If you love being outdoors in nature then you could be a wildlife biologist. There are so many interesting jobs with animals that there is something to suit everyone.

Five things you couldn't do without animals

- Drink milk
- Wear clothes made of wool
- Go riding
- Visit zoos
- Have pets

Animal job chart

If you want to find out more about any of the jobs in this book, start here:

	Animal care assistant	Animal welfare inspector	Assistance dog trainer	Entomologist	
You need to:	Know how to look after pets	Care about how animals are treated	Be patient and love dogs	Love bugs	
Best thing about it:	Finding new owners for rescue pets!	Rescuing animals from danger!	Seeing a dog help its new owner!	Discovering something new about insects!	

	Farmer	Police dog handler	Riding instructor	Vet	Wildlife biologist	Zookeeper
	Be able to get out of bed early	Care for your dog for many years	Be a good teacher	Be good at talking to people	Be able to concentrate for a long time	Know how to care for all types of animals
	Being out in the countryside!	Working with your best friend!	Working with horses every day!	Saving animals' lives!	Seeing rare animals in the wild!	Spending every day with amazing animals!

Glossary

conservation protecting Earth and living things from pollution or damage

emergency situation that needs fast action

expert person who knows a lot about something

habitat a plant or animal's natural environment

handle touch or move something carefully using hands

injured hurt or damaged

laboratory place where scientists do experiments or study things closely

visually impaired having partial or no sight

volunteer person who works or helps without pay

Find out more

RSPCA
www.rspca.org.uk
Visit the RSPCA website to find out more about caring for animals and the people who work with them.

ZSL London Zoo
www.zsl.org/education/keepers-diary/
Visit this website to read a zookeeper's diary!

Blue Cross
www.bluecross.org.uk
This charity's website has plenty of information about caring for animals.

The Bug Club
www.amentsoc.org/bug-club/
Find out more about being an entomologist at this website.

Index

animal care assistants 20–21, 28

animal welfare inspectors 18–19, 28

assistance dog trainers 24–25, 28

chickens 8

conservation 5, 11, 17

cows 8

dogs 5, 14–15, 21, 24–25, 28, 29

emergencies 19

entomologists 12–13, 26, 28

experts 13, 17

farmers 8–9, 29

habitats 16, 17

health 6, 9, 11, 18, 20

horses 22–23, 29

importance 4–5, 27

insects 12–13, 26, 28

llamas 8

medicines 6

Olympics 22

ostriches 8

police dog handlers 14–15, 29

rescue animals 19, 21, 28

riding instructors 22–23, 29

sheep 8

teaching 13, 23, 29

training 15, 21, 22, 24, 25

vets 6–7, 29

volunteers 24

wildlife biologists 16–17, 27, 29

zookeepers 10–11, 29